WILTED FLOWERS & STRAIGHT JACKETS

wilted flowers & straight jackets

musings of a melodramatic

ERICKA GARRAFFA

i wanted to hate you, but i've never known how, so i wrote you into immortality instead, because that is what i know.

the words on these pages will stay here longer than you know how to.

consider this a content warning and a trigger warning.
enjoy!

they once named a hurricane after me
and before that day i had never felt so seen
i am all harsh winds and destruction
the eye of the storm never lasts long enough to hold
you say it's whirlwind
i say find somewhere safe and take cover
once the dust settles
and the smoke clears
you will understand why
they once named a hurricane after me

i knew i would not be okay once you left me again
from previous experiences i knew this one would hurt like hell
but you forgot to take your memory with you
you left your laughter behind, still ringing in my ears
the brightness in your eyes
the smile that never met my lips
your voice that still echoes in everything i do
and your face that still haunts me every night in my dreams

-*ghosts do exist*

when you came back you promised me it would be different
you promised me you would stay
you promised you had changed
you begged for forgiveness
you begged for me to let you back in
you begged for mercy
but here i sit, three months later
10 years later
waiting for you to make one goddamn promise
you won't break the way you broke me

-cold hearted promises

i am just the shell of a girl without you here

-empty

there is a casual cruelty in the ways you've come back to me
home and heartache dancing through me with ease
i always held that hopeless hope close to my chest
always kept just enough empty space somewhere inside me
no matter how full my life felt
and at some point i accepted that that's all it would ever be
hopeless and empty
but i've been blindsided by the return of you
and all the feelings that came rushing back with you
leaving me breathless and terrified and hopeful and new
but somehow more myself than i've been in so long
falling right back into step like we never lost a moment
like we never lost a thing
but the quiet heavy spaces between seconds remind us
we still have so much buried inside these shallow graves we carved
into our bones for each other

-uncovering

you showed up at an old friend's funeral
and i couldn't help but wonder if you'd have the audacity to show
your face at mine
would you still be in disbelief
even though you saw this coming the first time you saved me from
it
would you put on a show and tell everyone how close we used to
be
will you tell them the story of the time i loved you and you loved
me back
and will you leave out all the parts about you leaving and breaking
my heart
will you forget to mention that i begged for your love to stay
only to have you act like i was a stranger when we ran into each
other
will you tell them how you said you couldn't stand the thought of
losing me the night i tried to die
then you were gone by sunrise the next morning
i bet you forget to remember all the hell you put me through so no
one questions if these are your initials carved into my casket
tell them how i clawed at your bones to keep you here
and all you did was twist out of my grip and run
make it known that you ruined a girl who only ever knew how to
care for you unconditionally
and now she's gone and you can't apologize
i hope you're up late tossing and turning because you can't get me
out of your head
and you finally understand what it's like to be me

i hope you have sleepless nights spent begging god to bring me
back to you
drowning in hopelessness because you were too late
i hope you get the news when you're having a good time
and you can't find a bathroom quick enough to purge your regrets
i hope your hands shake and your eyes stay bloodshot
from the restlessness and memories you see so perfectly all of a
sudden
i hope this loss distracts you from reality so badly that your mother
calls you every night to make sure you're eating enough
i hope you see how much you've hurt me in the purple bags under
my eyes that the makeup couldn't hide
i hope you lose your mind in the middle of a crowded street corner
and fall to your knees asking god for mercy
and to let you see me alive one last time
oh but you'll be too late
and you'll regret wasting all the chances i gave that you never
deserved
i hope it eats you alive
and I'll sit back and watch you go insane from a place where it
doesn't hurt to love you anymore
-untitled 2014

i once lost a love that was more than love
i stood tall in that loss
and tried to cling to the pieces you left behind
i left trails of paper flowers and pretty words behind me
as i navigated my way through the dark
so that maybe you would find your way back to me someday
i was never meant to hold you
you've always been such a pretty little untouchable thing
only able to reach out and feel you in my dreams and thoughts and
words
with every passing moment and every outstretched hand ignored
you put more and more distance between me and my hopeless
hopes
i neatly folded all i had left of you
and tucked it away into your shallow grave
where you had no choice but to return to
only bringing you flowers on your birthday and the day i had to say
goodbye

-*revival*

burying love alive is the easiest way to become a dead man walking
it's hard to navigate grief when you don't die with it
you only attend the funeral and visit the grave when you've had too
much to drink
and you're always so goddamn drunk
the haunting always feels like the hardest part
the ghosts that linger inside of you
they pass through every wall of the haunted house you have let
yourself become
uncovering past lives and reviving dead ends and reliving all those
tiny little deaths you had to fight so hard to survive
allowing the dead man walking to stumble back into your life
trying not to drown in all the tears you never let yourself cry until
now
bringing the dead back to life is the hardest part of love dying out

-apocalypse

i forgot how the song goes
i remember how it starts and i remember how it ends
but somewhere in the middle the lines blur and run together
and i can't make out the words
as the melodies and maladies begin to fade from my mind
i start learning the words to new songs and the steps to new dances
and i spend every day putting on my best show and breaking both
legs
but there is a distant ringing in my ears that reminds me that this is
all performative
and the stage only exists because people want to see me fall off of it
but i don't stumble until i see your face making its way through the
crowd again
the familiarity of you made the record scratch
and now all i know is the beginning
the middle
and the new end to our old favorite song
so please get on this stage with me and sing beside me
til we are both breathless and on the floor laughing in that all too
comfortable way
that tells everyone in the audience that this is the only song we've
ever truly known
and that we've spent all this time apart humming the tune in
grocery stores
and on sidewalks
and with never enough lovers who will never recognize the sound
we will never forget
-singing in the rain

thinking of you lately leaves me speechless
breathless most days
how many funerals have i held for you?
planning another funeral for a ghost
who has somehow clawed their way out of the dirt I've already
buried them in
how many little black dresses can one girl own?
i'm running out of outfits to lay you to rest in
and words to speak as your eulogy
maybe i'll wear the dress from my birthday
the one you'd recognize even in the afterlife
a black dress for a celebration,
in hindsight feels almost like foresight
like i should have seen this ending coming the same way it has
before
i don't want to keep mourning you like this
i don't want to keep missing you like this
the ink doesn't even have time to dry anymore before i am making
arrangements again
how many tears does it take
to flood the earth and bring you back here one last time?
how many empty prayers to a sky full of you does it take to bring
you back to life?
i'm crying with the moon and screaming these dreams of you
and hoping to run into your ghost again
maybe in the next lifetime you'll come back as someone who can
love me

-haunted

i'm feeling sunbleached
drowning myself in light
and afraid of the dark
here, hold this lighter version of me
because the dark will swallow both of us whole
engulfed in warmth
rekindled flame
both hiding third degree burns from a spark that never truly died
out
when the heart is in a drought
it takes nothing to start a forest fire
that consumes our entire corner of this lifetime
so burn with me
burn with me bright enough to show everyone around us
that ending in a pile of ash is worth the heat of our touch

-*rekindling*

my body is full of a distant late winter
my bones stiff and chattering from the stark cold i was left in
but it was spring just two months ago
love blooming at the tip of your tongue
warm and new but decades old and sturdy too
but i have made a home of these bare trees and grey skies by now
sharp winds split my skin wide open
and i'm left to purge all that you left behind in this second coming
of all the violent ways i could have survived you
mourning your resurrection in silence is the cruelest thing i've
allowed myself to endure
i keep a small flame of hope inside me,
that the sun may show its face again soon
and flowers may start to bloom
but still nothing
and breaking frozen ground only leaves my knuckles bloody and
knees bruised,
not enough to keep me warm
so i pray this avalanche buries me alive
like i had to bury you

-frozen in time

fall into me
just once
fall into me
take your paperweight heart off your sleeve
fall into me
lay it all at my feet
fall into me
together we can grieve
all the ways that this life has been daunting and unkind
fall into me
and i promise you will never search for another place to rest

i carry grief around with me like it is my name
my parents gave it to me when i was born
and i've been trying to find a way to make this birthright less heavy
ever since
at some point i got used to the constant pressure
but it lurks in the shadows and windsong and words of the ones
around me
and i'm back on my knees
begging for an outstretched hand to share the weight
and help me back to my feet
i will carry this grief with me,
the nametag so clearly written on my face,
until i can be beside you again

to think that sweaters are made entirely of knots
but the knots in my stomach when i saw you with her
were not good enough for sweaters
instead they made me want to burn every stitch of my clothing you
have ever touched

-relighting old flames

tell me, can you breathe under all the love i've smothered you with?
all i have ever wanted
was for someone to hold my rough hands
as softly as you have
to make me feel like all of my wholehearted attempts at being
enough
have not gone to waste
but the color of your eyes don't compare
to the blue that washed over me when i lost you
take these flowers as you leave
plant them in the sun
come may, i hope they bloom the words you haven't said in so long

-may 11th

who would've guessed
the light i was blind to
would be the reason i'm sitting here in flames tonight
the wild eyed wild hearted one
with a finger on the trigger and a love that is always on the run
i beg you to sit still for a moment
catch your breath
maybe stay a while
but i know better than to try to cage the wind
and i'm not naive enough to think i can make it change direction
so i will just sit in this heat
let it burn
and feel the wind all around me
knowing it will only fan these flames
and i will never truly be able to hold it

-gone with the wind

born to be a lover girl
forced to be the one who got away
so i got away

lately i have been consumed by grief
heavy in the chest
and a heart bleeding down the sleeve of my favorite shirt
reaching so desperately for a hand to keep me steady
while running from anyone reaching back for me
bringing flowers to everyone i love
because i am a funeral inside
everyone deserves flowers before they become their own funeral

-a eulogy

seems all i know how to do is fall apart in your presence
you could break me over and over again
and i would still pick up the shattered pieces
and put them back in your hands until i turn to dust
use me
hurt me
take all the pain you refuse to feel
and make me feel it
i want you to break me
over and over and over again
let me down
kick me while I'm bleeding out on the floor
i don't fucking care
as long as i can pretend to have you here for another moment
as long as i can pretend you love me
make me feel like you need me
then knock me off cloud nine
pretend you're standing with outstretched arms waiting to catch
me
then step out of the way at the last second
hurt me
break me
build me up just to throw it all to the ground again
i do not care
as long as it feels like i can hold you here in this lifetime
just a little bit longer
i don't care
just don't leave me here alone

please don't ask me to trust you when i am still coughing up water
from the last time you let me drown

yes i know its over and yes i know nothing i could do in a thousand
years could ever change it but holy fuck i'm not over it i'm not i have
to have closure from everything that has led me to open wounds and i
just cannot seem to find it
i have been searching for some kind of goddamn bandage for all
this bleeding that everyone swore would be temporary because "time
heals all wounds" but i am still fucking bleeding
and maybe i haven't given these wounds enough time to heal but if
i don't see a scab or a scar forming soon i swear i am going to drown
in all of this bloodletting and still have to take the blame for fucking
up everything because instead of opening my mouth to say something
i try so hard to open my fucking veins to bleed you out of me so that
maybe one day i will survive this

-leaving bones exposed

i broke down my own walls to let you in and you used my bricks to
build a wall around you and her
you held me close but her heart was small enough to get in be-
tween us
and her nails were sharp enough to rip you away from me
you were here for me to lean on when i couldn't hold myself up
but even the strongest beams can't support a weight so heavy
i cried an ocean of tears so i could drown
and from the bottom i could see you and her splashing on the
surface
i learned to use the spaces between breaths to fill the void
and i was doing fine until you came back to suffocate me
you put my life to a melody
and now i can't listen to the radio for fear of forgetting how we
sounded
i search for you in crowded places
but i can never find you because you're always hidden in her
shadows
she broke your heart and you begged for mercy
but she's not the god you made her out to be and i know how you
feel
she is to you what you are to me
you run to me for help but you can't find me in the chaos you left
behind
i am buried beneath shattered memories and broken pieces of
myself
and you've never been the kind to dig
until she used her claws to rip the ground from under us and
handed you a shovel to finish

Adele and i both know i must have called a thousand times
but you can't hear anything other than her broken record voice
we have both moved on from our past
but i still torture myself with occasional visits that last far too long
you look right past me but i know you and i know me
and that's why my heart sinks every time you pretend i'm not there
if i could turn back time
i'd turn these disconnections into reconnections
and show you just what you were going to do to me
your regrets are blinded by her light
and i wear mine on my body like battle wounds from fighting the
urge to need you

-disconnections

let's talk about how saving me is a constant battle and you're ready
for war
let's talk about how you only feel at home when you're furthest
from it
let's talk about the way my mind wanders to the memories you've
all but taken with you
let's talk about the way you touched me for the first time and
seared your name into my bones
let's talk about how your absence is so heavy it feels like presence
let's talk about how we lived through so many seasons together
and now that you're gone again it is always winter
let's talk about the way my heartbeat hesitates when your kiss
meets mine
and i have never prayed for a heart attack until now
let's talk about how i never had intentions of staying in a place i'm
not welcome but loving you is home to me
let's talk about the way my veins ache when i think about you
let's talk about how i can't stop the world
but if i could capture stars and make a constellation that resembles
you, i would
can we talk about the way i'm willing to die for so many things
but i am willing to live for your love
can we talk

-little talks

i just feel empty and i'm forgetting how to turn that into poetry

what the fuck is the point of an invisible string
if it is going to snap under the slightest pressure
your leaving is always so goddamn violent
in the quietest of ways
leave it to fire signs to leave you reeling
and aching to burn it all to the ground
but you're just a cowardly little lion
with a heart of steel and spine of aluminum foil
folding under any weight
strangling me with the invisible string
while you retreat to comfort
cheers to another decade of begging gods i don't believe in
for some kind of fucking reason as to why
i can never fucking hold you here

-invisible string

i'm tossing and turning and can't catch my breath
i'm tangled in my sheets and my hair is matted and my pillow
drenched with sweat
and i can hear myself screaming
and i can feel hands trying to shake me out of it
but the dreams you choose to show yourself in are so comfortably
painful
that i am afraid to wake up because that is the only time i can see
you
and i don't know if sleeping or being awake is the part that is
supposed to be the nightmare

-*don't wake me up*

i want to forgive you
like i did all those years ago
when you left me with no real reason
and no apology to heal the things that broke that cold late winter
morning

your return was unexpected
enough to turn my whole world upside down
uncover your shallow grave
bring you back to life
after a decade of mourning
a decade of pretending i know how to live without the comfort of
you
but you left me the same way you did the first time
abandonment with no remorse

and I've always been told to believe people the first time they show
you who they are
but this is not who you are
who you are deserves forgiveness
understanding and unconditional love
but the person you've become
the one you're pretending to be
does not deserve forgiveness
no mercy rule in this sick game you've started
knowing the odds were always stacked against me
you deserve the anger
the rage

the sadness
to know the truth, the aftermath, the chaos and the aftershock
of having to learn to survive you a second time

-the second coming

as much as it hurts
as bad as i want to scream until my lungs collapse
and collapse into this nothingness you have left here with me
and as desperately as i need to cry until i throw up
and talk about what you did until i have no choice but to rip my
own vocal cords out
i am lucky
i am so lucky to have known a love like this
something beyond time and distance
something beyond this lifetime
to have known something so precious to me
that losing it breaks my every bone
and shakes me to my very core
turns me into something unrecognizable, quiet
a loss i may never truly recover from
it is just the love left behind for a soul that could never be replaced
i am lucky i got the time i did
i am lucky to hold these moments
and these memories so close to my chest
i will visit them when i need to be drenched in light
when the grey skies of missing you become too heavy

-lucky number 13

making a mess out of me and leaving me where i shattered
returning only to check on this chaos from the shadows
lighting matches just to see how long they burn
setting fires in my favorite meadow just to watch it all disappear
dropping lit cigarettes into oil spills just to see how far destruction
will trail
playing russian roulette with thunderstorms just to see if getting
struck by lightning scars over just like getting too close to you
getting struck by lighting again because i believed too hard in it
never striking the same place twice
waiting right where you left me hoping to be struck a third time
hoping for the weather to feel the same as your presence in my
mind
so that maybe i can feel like you're close to me one last time
before i let you run with the wind like you always fucking do

-come in with the rain

you've become that sweet spot between midnight and isolation
and I'm dancing on the edge of not ever again
regrets collect like old friends to relive my darkest moments
like a little girl afraid of the monster under her bed
except i am the monster and i am under the bed
and i am afraid of what i've become in your absence
i was more than this once
and now i'm waves on rocky shoreline
drowning in this crash course in losing touch with reality
and this is not poetry anymore
this is me begging you to come back through the tip of a pen
but there are no more pretty words
just the constant and lingering thought of you
and your absence being so heavy that it feels like presence

-aftershock

i don't pity you
pity is insulting
please know that when i say my heart breaks for you
it is because i know that same pain all too well
i see the dead inside look in your eyes
and recognize it like my reflection in a mirror
i hear the screaming in your silence
i feel how heavy the empty is in my chest
even though it's not my ache to carry
i know you feel like you haven't held it long enough
but it weighs so much
and you already have the rest of the world
resting on your shoulders
i'd like to hold some of it for you
i will sit beside you in the dark
offering a safe place to lay it all down for a moment of honesty
take your armor off and bleed where you need to
i'm not afraid of the dark
and your mess is not an inconvenience
your heavy heart is not a burden here
this is a safe place to shatter

-savior complex

this loss made me go silent
the only thing i know to do is ache
allow the pain its rightful space to course through me bone deep
to sit statuesque in warm moments gone too soon
i want to scream and cry and write and break
but no sound knows how to escape me this time
leaving distance and concern between me and my loved ones
but it is hard to pretend to be human
when you are nothing but an open wound
bleeding out onto everything and everyone you touch
but i will still pick at this decade old scab
because if it ever fully heals
there is nothing left of you here
rose petal bandages sitting in graveyards
to memorialize a life we almost had
and so i will tuck this wilted flower
into the crevices of this straight jacket
that holds me inside the lovely little loneliness you have left me in
so that maybe i won't feel so far from you

-wilted flowers & straight jackets

i love you more than the ways you are always so fleeting
but one day i will wake up
and my first thought will not be you
i know because i have had to survive you before
you were never my sun my moon and all my stars
you were just my person
and sometimes that's just not enough
goodbye-kissing lips i never got to taste
still wrapped up in soft eulogies
like the last of the leaves holding to autumn trees
this is the ache of healing
the chaos of longing
my chest heavy with homesickness for a home this lifetime will
never let me know
plucking flower petals to see how long you'll love me this time
dandelion wishes of nothing i can ever hold
late spring love bloomed in your mouth
and died in my chest before summertime's close
i've spent lifetimes loving you and losing you in every season
i'm used to the cold that has crept its way back in
but i am chilled to the bone
and the loss of you has frozen me to my core
and if i have to learn to live without you again
i pray your future loves you more than i ever could

-*tis the season*

sometimes the world spins a little too fast
days slip past me in my two steps forward one step back
feeling like i'll never keep up, never catch up
suddenly it was spring and the world came to a screeching halt
a directional change
a shift i couldn't steady my feet quick enough for
before i knew it everything was spinning backwards
until i found myself as a 15 year old girl
who knew no better at the time
but to love you with all she had
loving you always felt like running full speed ahead
no steps backwards
no brakes no stopping no slowing until i reached the destination,
you
the world started spinning forward again until i was a 16 year old
girl
and there was another screeching halt
except this time it was us
coming to an unexpected end
an impact i could have never braced for
and all i knew after that moment was cold and unforgiving floors
sometimes the world spins a little too fast
and we get left behind
but i started to pick up the pace with my two steps forward one
step back
until i was far enough from the loss of you
far enough from the loss of me
that it all became shadows in the dark
and i was in a new world

spinning just fast enough to keep me dizzied
one step forward, ten years back
now the world has passed me by so quickly
that there is no solid ground to find my footing again
i am reeling and unraveling and raging
clawing at the sides of the earth
handfuls of soft ground falling away
as i try not to fall away with it
playing keep up is collapsing my lungs
and my knuckles are bloodied and raw
from grasping at nothing solid enough to hold me
sometimes the world spins too fast
and two steps forward, one step back is not enough to keep me
from falling
dizzy and breathless

-spinning out of control

i have so much of you in my heart
and now you're leaving me
what do i do with all of this?
there is nowhere it can go
i cannot set it down or push it away
i can't let you go
where do i go now?
you're the only home i know
how do i fool myself and everyone else into believing i'm okay?
my heart has shattered
and decorates the floor around my feet
do i run from these memories?
do i stand in one place
holding hope with white knuckles that you'll realize your mistake?
will you ever come back?
will you ever find a place to settle in here
will i ever learn to be okay without you here?

-unrequited

grateful for the present of presence
but terrified of the meaning of it
i'm not sure why you're here
or how long it may last
so i will not take it for granted
and i will carefully tuck each moment away
so that if this ends again too soon
i'll have enough of you to carry with me until the next lifetime
every word on these pages has always been me begging for another
chance to hold you a little longer
and now that you've been written back into my life
i am afraid that i will follow your lead
and run as far as i can
from the warmth of this sacred home

-gifts

you're casually answering questions in conversation
that i screamed into the oblivion of your absence
it comes out as a joke
but the laughter you hear is just me trying to catch my breath
you told me that i take up all of the space in your mind
like the walls inside my head haven't been painted to match the
blue of your eyes for the last 14 years
and i am always forgetting to redecorate in here
you said you feel like you hung up the best version of yourself ten
years ago
and you're not sure you will ever have that back
i promised i would let you back in
but i realize now, in your leaving this place again, that you were
not just saying you miss us
but warning me that you could never come back here to stay
i try not to be so angry at your sweet nothing promises
but i don't know if I'll ever understand
why you had to come visit after a decade away from home
just to leave for foreign lands without so much as goodbye this
time
-*sweet nothings*

part of me will always wonder what if
but the other part of me is okay with accepting what is
because i know that we once shared a world together
and i can always visit that world in my mind
when my heart starts searching for you again
the memories are always just as warm as the moments were
and i'd be okay with crawling inside of one
and dying there

it's the "what ifs" right?
what ifs can drive you
absolutely
undoubtedly
undeniably mad
you wake up to someone new each morning
but never the right someone
you fall asleep next to a strange new body each night
but never the right somebody
always wondering
always questioning
what if it was the right one
instead of all these wrongs
spending countless nights looking in all the wrong places for all the
right answers
what if?
what if i told you that you had the right one
you already found her
but you let her go too soon
because you weren't ready
or because you were scared
or she didn't look how you imagined the right one to look
what if everything you wanted and needed
hoped for begged for prayed for
was right there in front of you begging for your heart and soul
and you let it all go
and what if you came crawling back
begging and pleading for a second chance
that you never even wanted the first time

what if you apologized and cried
and laid out all your achings on the line for her to reconsider
what if i told you
you're just too late
you can't have something back that you didn't want when you had
it
what if i told you
sometimes there is no second chance
and sometimes you have to give your all the first time around
or lose it all
what if it's over
what if i never let you back in
what if you gambled with something you couldn't afford to lose
and now you're broke

and i think one of the hardest parts
is sitting with this stupid little feeling i get
when i remember
you love like moonlight
and i only know how to love like rain
i love like heavy
i love like consuming
i love like falling
and you're the ground waiting to catch me
and you
you only know how to love in phases
-*moons ago*

we tell them they'll never understand
and i'm starting to think i've become one of them
your leaving leaves me lost and longing
wondering who and where and why
and what the fuck is so wrong with keeping you close
and why i can never seem to do it
i just can't understand what i did
to deserve your reckless abandons
time and time again
when all i wanted
was to see you here again

i can't quite find the words to paint the right picture
of just how small and bruised you've made me feel
you always build me up
just to let me right back down
the freefall back to reality always leaves me winded and shattered
like I've been pushed down and trampled
an endless barrage of being crushed under the weight of empty
spaces
like a child losing their mother in a crowded place
like falling down a cliffside
like I'm the butt of the cruelest joke
a twisted and sickening game i never agreed to play
like being asked out as a joke
and hearing the laughter erupt from behind you after saying yes
i feel naive and embarrassed and just so stupid
they say if something feels too good to be true
it usually is
it is
it always is
and i still believed in you

there is a version of me somewhere out there who has never met
you
i'd like to think of her as featherlight and warm
i'm hopeful that she does not know this kind of loss
this kind of aching
i wonder if she has her own version of you, sometimes
i wonder if she has a better version of you, sometimes
i wonder if there is a version of this story that lets us get it right for
once
i wonder how free she is
and how full her life might feel
and if she never knows you
she never knows the weight of the empty place inside of us
i carry it alone
alongside some envy for her
though I'm not sure she's the true winner here
because it is not the knowing you that hurts
it is not the loving you that hurts
it's the losing you
the learning to live again without you that hurts
when you are here
it is all warmth and laughter and familiarity
drenched in golden light
and then you leave
and i feel like i have never known the sun
losing you is self destruction
and having you here is knowing myself better than ever before
of course it hurts
but the version of me who never met you

will never understand the love she missed out on
-better version

don't you dare come back here and try to kill me when i couldn't do
it myself
don't you fucking dare blow in with a stiff wind of chaos
to unearth everything i play pretend buried to survive your
abandonings
i had to bury you alive
surviving you always feels like dying
i had to mourn you in ways you can't call mourning
i buried you and you haunted my every moment after
i learned to make peace with your ghost
and the warmth of familiarity
safe and sound here in this memory of you
now you're a dead man walking
abandoned ship, instead of going down with it
like i do every time
you become the iceberg I'm crashing into
how dare you push until i caved
how dare you crash into me
and run again
like you don't know you're fleeing the scene of a tragic fucking
accident

-a wreck

TOD:
10 years, 3 months, 6 days.

we deserved a better ending each time we ended
i deserved more than what you were too afraid to give
i am raging and desolate and heavy
but i don't have much to say anymore
tired of spinning circles
so i will spin my wheels
until this is all just dust settling behind me
and let the gods i never believed in handle the rest
i pray and ask them to spare you
begging to have some mercy on you for the things you've done
here
for you are not wicked
just afraid of things that love fiercely
though karma may have other plans
she rarely consults the gods when doing her due diligence
and she can't hear my pleadings to this sky so full of you
i have never wanted you to have all that you deserve
more than i do now
-final acts of love

i always dreamed of resilience
of surviving tragedy without losing myself too
but i have always been too sensitive for that version of survival
i bend and i break and i scream and i cry
until i have let enough out of me
so that it becomes something i can carry
but i hardened under that last loss
the weight of it, something I'll never have the strength to hold
it took something big from me
it took something vital out of me
rough edges grow where softness once lived
venom coursing through me so violently that i spill onto everyone
around me
and i never learned to let go with grace
my love has always been claws and teeth
nothing has ever gotten away whole
especially not myself
i am soft words and sharp edges and sealed lips and passionate
kisses from dead lovers
i lose more of me every day
the people i bleed for always take the best pieces of me with them
when they go
a blessing
and a curse
that is always shared equally

-*graceless*

your absence carries a weight that convinces me you're still here in
this room with me
almost like you never left
almost
but sometimes a sadness is larger than the heart that has to carry it
and here i crumble
with a heart so abandoned
only ghosts dare to take up residence
and the rain never stops these days
i've learned to love it more than the sun
because I'm sure it is the sky saying it misses you here too
the underside of joy is sorrow
and when it shows itself
like the soft white underbelly of a leaf in the wind
it rains
i am drowning in grief
i am drowning in memories and words
spoken and unspoken
and regrets
and you and you and you and you and you
you were supposed to stay this time
and i have a feeling the end of the world is going to look a lot like
the inside of my heart when you left me

-rain rain, don't go away

how many pages of i miss yous and i love yous and i think i hate
yous can i write
before i bleed this pen and myself dry
i just ache so deeply for a love i almost knew
and i am forgetting how to turn that into poetry
i can only do so much with these words
before i am just on my knees and begging you to love me enough to
stay for once
-ink stains

write to turn the messes into masses
write to purge this awful taste from my mind
bleeding myself dry onto these pages
every line is your name
letter by letter
write to remind myself that, through the anger and aching, it was
important
and it was beautiful while i got to hold it
i can't stop watching the ink dry
knowing each pen stroke keeps your memory here another
moment longer
write to remember what it was
write to remember what it almost was
but almost only counts in horseshoes and hand grenades
and your destruction has always been more than almost
write to let you go
write to bring you back to me
someday i hope these pens bleed out
and there are no more pages left for me to scream into
because sometimes the ink is just a metaphor
for what is stagnating in my veins
each time my heart beats to the rhythm of losing you
there is something so delicate in dressing up goodbyes as poetry

-dried ink pleadings

clawing at your bones to keep you here
going to war to fight this loss
losing myself to the battle of saving something that never existed
outside of us
i am stubborn enough to fight for your place here
but i am not stupid enough to believe you'll ever stay
this connection will always be a beautiful and distant lifetime we
lost
but I'm waving my white flag
surrendering to the loss of my greatest friend
my purest love
my kindest and cruelest pieces of my life
surrendering to your always temporary lifetimes here with me
surrendering the fight to keep my head above water
letting loss fill my lungs and sink me
because i will rise again
and you will have no place here when i do
the phoenix does not go back to sift through the ashes it rose from

they always talk about the storm
the mess that it left in its wake
after all the rain has flooded
after all the down trees
no one talks about the clean up
the aftermath, the after mess, the aftershock
they only search for rainbows in a sky that is still black
ignoring the damage left behind
i never know how to survive losing you
the sky stayed black today
but the air was not quiet
like the rest of the earth isn't quite sure how to survive me losing
you either
the sun rises like it is shy of showing its face
knowing the darkness it will battle when it wakes for another day
birds will hum instead of sing
flowers hardly half bloom
it is always raining
and i am drenched in this new old grief
does the thunder ever stop rolling
will i drown in this downpour
will i ever find the words to talk about the clean up
the aftermath, the after mess, the aftershock
-all we know of love is how to destroy it

most days i can't tell the difference between the world giving me a
sign
and torturing me with memories
and i fear nostalgia for the ways it can make a nightmare seem
pleasant to be stuck in
and i fear the ways you love me
and the ways you let me go so effortlessly
suffocate me with words you'll never say
and teach me how to beg for your staying without rolling over in
my grave
after all, the best way to leave is to stay
i am stuck somewhere between mercy and merciless
somewhere between understanding and unforgiving
one day your name will not ache in my veins
but for now you are the only pain i have ever felt
and I'll lift myself up so i can taste the sky
i'll be alright i'll be alright i'll be alright

nothing changes the weight of the grief
no amount of talking screaming crying breaking running away
will ever lighten the load
and it does not feel like baggage
but i am chained to it
at the wrist, not the ankle
nothing will ever change the weight of this grief
but one day i will be strong enough to carry it instead of drag it
until then I'll follow the shattered flowers
and keep seeing how far i can bend before i break
and I'm turning out my pockets
finding the tiniest scraps of strength

those 'fucks me up every time' moments
but only with you, thinking of you, loving you
and losing you

dreaming of you never gets old
seeing your face when i don't expect it always leaves me warmer
than i was falling asleep
in my dreams i can run my hands through your hair
you kiss the bridge of my nose
and you hold my face with both hands
in my dreams you do not leave me
in my dreams you do not hurt me
the light in your eyes never dims in my dreams
the love never fades
when i wake up
i remember you are not here anymore
when i wake up
i am wearing how much i miss you all over me
but i don't want lonely where forever should've been
but these are just dreams at the end of a dusty road
where hearts and hands met
and never looked back
-day dreaming

if ever you get the urge to pick up that phone and reach for me
then reach
i have not moved an inch from the place you left me
i am still right here
waiting
hoping
wishful thinking
maybe someday you'll walk through that door again
but only if i leave it unlocked
so i will slam the door closed
but i will not lock it
a small act of hope
a quiet act of love
a sad act of longing
but you will always hold space here
even if bridges go up in flames
the house on the other side of it has sturdy bones
-*good bones*

the sinking feeling in my chest
the way I'm left gasping for air
when the thought of you haunts me in my waking hours
i can't find the words to make you understand
the hole left in me
i was doing okay
spent the last few years building a life you never knew
a real life without your ghost here every day
but you came back
and turned me into a haunted house
the ghost of you knocks on my chest
and when i let it in there is no room left for air inside my lungs
sometimes i feel anxious
and i wonder if you're thinking of me in those moments
your ghost keeps me company when you're away
he holds your place
and keeps it warm until your hopeful return
and if you never do find your way back
at least your ghost doesn't know how to abandon me
-*favorite haunting*

if you had asked me 5 years ago
5 months ago
if i ever thought i'd see you again
speak to anyone other than your ghost again
i would have laughed myself to tears
no way that dream would come to life
i gave up on that almost a decade ago
and didn't dare let myself slip into an alternate reality where i could
let those thoughts run wild
you see, losing you changed me as a person
my chemical makeup was altered in this loss
but here we are
surviving the wreckage of dreams that were never supposed to
come true
and it was at first
a dream, that is
you said you were reintroduced to an angel
that i took up every part of of your mind
and you did the same for me
i just don't understand why you can't take up more than that
it was all so beautiful
so good
so refreshing to hold you here again so softly
now it's dark and heavy and makes me fucking nauseous
take me back to 5 years ago
to 5 months ago
when all i knew was the distant memory of you

you dug up this grave
and left my corpse laying
no flowers and no goodbye
no respect for the dead
i thought this was a resurrection
a revival
of something that deserved more than its untimely death
and now your cruel joke has left me exposed
and dying another thousand tiny little deaths
reliving what should have been
and reeling in all that haunts me in this afterlife
one day it will be my turn to haunt you
-*hoax*

you said i had my mind made up from our first conversation
but you don't know how wrong you are
i made this decision when i was just a girl
and still
i have never been so sure of anything else
i only hesitated long enough to catch my breath
when you asked me if i will have you back
i knew you wouldn't stay
when you said you weren't leaving this time
and i let you in anyway
because you will always have a home here in this hollowed out
chest
i protested your leaving
until there was too much distance to keep reaching for you
every decision that leads to leaving has always been yours
i've been standing in the same place i met you
but it was never me who couldn't keep you
it is you who never knows how to stay
and you may never get it right
and i may never let you
i hope you ache with regret in each step you take away from me
you're retracing the same old steps out that door
but i never would have left you
not like that

i gained the weight of you
and then i lost it
you and my mind
i may never get either one back
but pretending i had both was enough
even if it never lasts

august comes in full of hope
an intense buzz
electricity in the air
but something so deeply lacking
so empty aching hollow
beautiful things are happening here
and you are not here to share it with me
so these beautiful things come in with their own grief
like they wish you were here too
and only adds to mine

before you left this place again
we couldn't figure out why you were ever here to begin with
we couldn't understand it
and no amount of bracing for impact
left me prepared to face your leaving
but i think i get it now
i think i know why
after 10 years of living life without you in it
why you found your way back here so suddenly
so that i remain soft
i have learned to remain soft in cruel situations
and this was my final test
the cruelest situation i have ever known
i'm struggling to remain soft
to scrub these callouses away as they form
i'm lashing out
distancing
dissociating
disappearing
hardening under that last loss
you took something with you this time
something I'll never get back
you are my greatest loss
and to you
i am just another casualty
caught in the crossfire
collateral damage in your war against yourself
and i need the armor
-softening

i cannot celebrate you
the way you went out of your way to celebrate me
i wish i did have it in me to crash your party
but just like every year before this one
know that on this day
i have remembered you
carried you with me each moment
held you softly in my hands
wondering
hoping
that today is your best day
and that nothing is missing
though i know there are voices you wish could sing along
and i selfishly hope i am one of them this year
and every year
-happy birthday